The Firebombing of Tokyo: The History of the U.S. Air Force's Most Controversial Bombing Campaign of World War II

By Charles River Editors

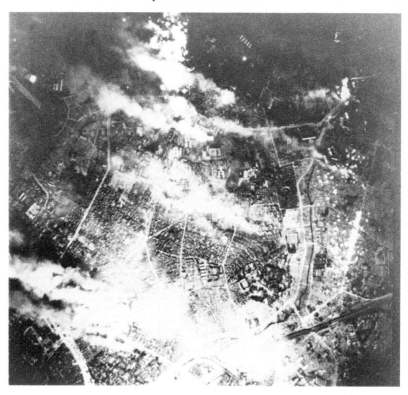

An aerial photo of Tokyo burning in May 1945

About Charles River Editors

Charles River Editors provides superior editing and original writing services across the digital publishing industry, with the expertise to create digital content for publishers across a vast range of subject matter. In addition to providing original digital content for third party publishers, we also republish civilization's greatest literary works, bringing them to new generations of readers via ebooks.

Sign up here to receive updates about free books as we publish them, and visit Our Kindle Author Page to browse today's free promotions and our most recently published Kindle titles.

Introduction

A picture of a neighborhood in Tokyo in the wake of the campaign

The Firebombing of Tokyo

"Maj. Gen. Curtis E. LeMay, commander of the B-29s of the entire Marianas area, declared that if the war is shortened by a single day, the attack will have served its purpose." – *The New York Times*,

Although it's often overlooked among histories of the Pacific, The first American air raid, the Doolittle raid, hit Tokyo in April 1942 as a symbolic response to the surprise attack against Pearl Harbor. The raid killed as many as 39 and came close to strafing the Imperial Palace, but compared to what was to come, the raid was light and haphazard. As American forces pushed the Japanese back across the Pacific from 1942-1944, their island-hopping campaign ultimately made it possible for the Air Force to conduct bombing runs over the Japanese mainland.

The first serious air raids came in November 1944, after the Americans had captured the

Marianas Islands, and through February 1945, American bombers concentrated on military targets at the fringes of the city, particularly air defenses. However, the air raids of March 1945, and particularly on the night of March 9, were a different story altogether. In what is generally referred to as strategic or area bombing, waves of bombers flew low over Tokyo for over two and a half hours, dropping incendiary bombs with the intention of producing a massive firestorm. The American raids intended to produce fires that would kill soldiers and civilians, as well as the munitions factories and apartment buildings of those who worked in them. 325 B-29s headed toward Tokyo, and nearly 300 of them dropped bombs on it, destroying more than 267,000 buildings and killing more than 83,000 people, making it the deadliest day of the war.

The firebombing that night and morning left 25% of Tokyo charred, with the damage spread out over 20 miles of the metropolis. In fact, the damage was so extensive that casualty counts range by over 100,000, as noted by Mark Selden in *Japan Focus*: "The figure of roughly 100,000 deaths, provided by Japanese and American authorities, both of whom may have had reasons of their own for minimizing the death toll, seems to be arguably low in light of population density, wind conditions, and survivors' accounts. With an average of 103,000 inhabitants per square mile (396 people per hectare) and peak levels as high as 135,000 per square mile (521 people per hectare), the highest density of any industrial city in the world, and with firefighting measures ludicrously inadequate to the task, 15.8 square miles (41 km2) of Tokyo were destroyed on a night when fierce winds whipped the flames and walls of fire blocked tens of thousands fleeing for their lives. An estimated 1.5 million people lived in the burned out areas."

Additional raids, this time largely on the north and west, came in April, and in May, raids hit Ginza and the south. Altogether, American bombers flew more than 4,000 missions over Tokyo before surrender. The damage was spread widely, but it was worst in the low city, where some neighborhoods were virtually depopulated as survivors fled to the relative safety of the countryside. Honjo and Fukagawa each lost roughly 95% of their pre-raid populations. In 1940, Tokyo was a city of perhaps 6.8 million, but two years after the end of the war, when the population had already begun to increase again, it was still no more than 4.1 million.

As with dropping the atomic bombs on Hiroshima and Nagasaki, the firebombing of Tokyo has remained controversial since the end of World War II. Japan had wisely spread out its industrial facilities across Tokyo so that one concerted attack could not deal a severe blow to its military capabilities. However, by spreading everything out, as the Germans had also done, Allied planes hit targets in residential zones, greatly increasing the casualties. Thus, by destroying as much of Tokyo's wartime manufacturing as possible, the American air force also destroyed half the city.

Of course, it's far easier with the advantage of hindsight for people to call the campaign disproportionate, especially since the bombing campaign came at a time when the United States still faced the dreadful prospect of invading Japan's mainland. In 2007, Japanese Prime Minister Abe Shinzō took responsibility for Japan's refusal to surrender when defeat was inevitable, thus placing the blame for the firebombing on Japan itself. Shinzō announced that Japan would financially compensate survivors and bereaved family members of those killed, and shortly after the announcement, 112 survivors filed a lawsuit seeking damages for damage done during the campaign.

The Firebombing of Tokyo: The History of the U.S. Air Force's Most Controversial Bombing Campaign of World War II chronicles the background of the campaign, its destruction, and its notorious legacy. Along with pictures of important people, places, and events, you will learn about the firebombing of Tokyo like never before, in no time at all.

The Firebombing of Tokyo: The History of the U.S. Air Force's Most Controversial Bombing Campaign of World War II

Chapter 1: Background

All Americans are familiar with the "day that will live in infamy." At 9:30 a.m. on Sunday, December 7, 1941, Pearl Harbor, the advanced base of the United States Navy's Pacific Fleet, was ablaze. It had been smashed by aircraft launched by the carriers of the Imperial Japanese Navy. All eight battleships had been sunk or badly damaged, 350 aircraft had been knocked out, and over 2,000 Americans lay dead. Indelible images of the USS *Arizona* exploding and the USS *Oklahoma* capsizing and floating upside down have been ingrained in the American conscience ever since. In less than an hour and a half the Japanese had almost wiped out America's entire naval presence in the Pacific.

The Americans would turn the war in the Pacific around in the middle of 1942, but in the wake of Pearl Harbor and the Japanese invasion of the Philippines, the country was in desperate need of a morale boost, and it would come in the form of the Doolittle Raid. In part to show that the Japanese were not invincible, and in part to reassure the American public that the nation would not lose the war, the Doolittle Raid included both Army and Navy units that launched 16 land-based medium bombers from an aircraft carrier, a feat that was the first of its kind but also one involving a great deal of risk. Getting the bombers and carriers in place to execute the mission involved much strategic planning and cooperation within the American military, and had it failed, it could have dealt a serious blow to the Americans' Pacific presence due to the nation's limited resources in that theater.

A picture of the bombers on deck on April 18 before the Doolittle Raid

A B-25B *Mitchell* taking off on the raid

As if getting in position wasn't challenging enough, the raid was never designed to include a round trip back to the carrier. Given the size of the bombers, the planes were unable to land back on the USS *Hornet*, so the plan was to have them fly over Japan and ditch in China after bombing Tokyo. While most of the crew would survive the mission, a few died during the raid, all of the planes were lost, and Japanese search parties eventually captured a number of Americans and executed three of them. One of the crews landed in the Soviet Union and would end up being interned there for a year.

From a tactical standpoint, the raid accomplished nothing of note, and Doolittle actually thought he would be punished for the results, but the Doolittle Raid served its purpose of boosting American resolve and demonstrating to the Japanese that they could be attacked at home as well. Furthermore, the Doolittle Raid showed the importance of air power in the war. It helped convince military planners of the power of a strong air force that could not only shift the balance of battles but could also hit military-industrial areas from long-range and thus cripple a nation's war-making abilities. The Japanese would take the capabilities of airplanes into account when formulating how to defend their empire, and it would help compel their leaders to make decisions such as the ones that led to the decisive Battle of Midway later in 1942.

Furthermore, in the aftermath of the Doolittle Raid of 1942, Japanese civilians began asking the government about how they could be protected against American bombs should another attack occur. Japanese civil defense leaders responded by telling civilians that they needed to build their own shelters. Civil defense authorities also advised people to build cisterns on their property, and they began safety programs to drill civilians in case of a possible attack.

A larger response to the dangers of American bombing missions did not materialize before the summer of 1944 because the official Japanese governmental position was that American aircraft could not reach the home islands. In actuality, the situation had changed in 1943 when the United States began producing the B-29 Superfortress, a super-bomber that had longer range than previous aircraft. B-29s were sent to China and India, but American war planners found out that the distance was still too far to attack important sites on the Japanese home islands, so they were limited to bombing Manchuria and Kyushu, the westernmost of the home islands.

B-29 Superfortress

In the fall of 1944, the distance between American air fields and the home islands shrank when B-29s were sent to the Marianas Islands, a new base from which to attack Japan, and that November, an attack by B-29 squadrons hit targets in Japan. With that, American governmental officials believed that "Tokyo's war industries have been badly hurt," and that "no part of the Japanese Empire is…out of range." (Hoyt, p.3) Three days later, B-29s hit Tokyo, though at this stage, the psychological impact of the bombing mission far outweighed its physical destruction.

A picture of B-29s dropping bombs on Tokyo

By early 1945, American military planners realized that they could bomb the Japanese home islands with impunity by flying at 20,000-30,000 feet because Japanese antiaircraft guns could not reach the bombers and Japanese fighters were not equipped for high-altitude missions. However, these tactics would change in February 1945 when General Curtis LeMay, the man who oversaw the bombing missions, began experimenting with the use of incendiary bombs and then with low-altitude incendiary bombing missions. These low-altitude missions would be designed to maximize the destruction of Japan.

LeMay

In order to understand the bombing missions in Japan, it necessary to understand the military technology that America developed in the aftermath of Pearl Harbor, which ultimately made it possible to undertake such an endeavor. Prior to 1940, the Army Air Corps focused on developing high-explosive bombs that would be focused on individual targets, but in 1940, the military experimented with their bombs by filling a chemical bomb casing that previously held an irritant gas with a mixture made up of rubber, lye, coconut oil, and gasoline already used by the British. The resulting mixture, which had the texture of a jelly, created an incendiary bomb that was designated the M-47. In 1941, the American military went a step further by acquiring not just the filler but an entire bomb. This bomb, the M-50, had a magnesium casing that was filled with powdered aluminum and iron oxide.

An M-47 bomb

An M-50 bomb

These two bombs would be used for different purposes. The M-47 was heavier at 100 pounds and therefore had better penetration capabilities, so this bomb would be used on large structures. For example, the M-47 would crash through a building's roof, and then a "burster charge would detonate, blowing the casing apart and dispersing flaming gobs of gasoline gel downward and outward in a conical pattern over a circle of about 60 feet under ideal conditions." (Kerr, p.12).

Conversely, the four pound M-50 was used on smaller buildings. The M-50 was dropped in clusters of 34 bombs, and after one of these groups of bombs fell, "an arming wire would release the metal bands that held the bombs, allowing them to separate during descent. After penetrating the roof and coming to rest, the filler mixture would ignite and its intense heat would then ignite the magnesium body. The ensuing fire would burn for about ten minutes at 2400 degrees Fahrenheit and was difficult to extinguish…" (Kerr, p.12).

While both of these bombs were used by the United States in World War II, American scientists also developed a third incendiary device that would be used quite prominently in the bombing raids against Japan. In September of 1941, Air Force General Henry Arnold wrote to Vannevar Bush, head of the Office of Scientific Research and Development, asking him to develop a substitute incendiary bomb because of a shortage of magnesium. Bush and his team from the National Defense Research Committee (NDRC) subsequently created two gasoline-gel fillers, and they also created a new bomb.

Arnold

Bush

This new M-69 bomb was small, since the Army Air Corps already had the 100 pound M-47 and wanted a replacement for the small M-50 bomb. The new bomb weighed 6.2 pounds, and, like the M-50, it would be dropped in clusters. However, what made it different from the M-50 is that once the bomb came to rest inside the target, a delay fuse would ignite, and after 3-5 seconds it would detonate an ejection-ignition charge. Upon detonation, "a TNT charge would explode, and magnesium particles would ignite the gasoline gel contained in a cloth sock. Unlike any other bomb, the explosion blew burning gel out of the tail of the casing and – like a miniature cannon – shot it as far as 100 feet. If the gel struck a combustible surface and was not extinguished it started an intense and persistent fire." (Kerr, p.14).

By 1942, American and British military officials were using these kinds of incendiary devices to bomb German cities in an attempt to reduce civilian morale. For example, when the British bombed the city of Cologne in May 1942, they used a mixture of high explosive and incendiary bombs to inflict as much damage as possible. Ultimately, the conclusion American military observers came to while analyzing the bombing missions in Europe was that "the clue to the successful all-out bombing of Germany lies more in the use of incendiaries than in high explosives…Even more vital, consequently, than the mere temporary dislocation of an industrial target through the use of H.E. [high explosive bombs] is the permanent fire destruction of the homes and essential services for Germany's war workers. These are, therefore, today regarded as the primary target for air attack. If the homes and essential services of Germany's war workers are destroyed through mass incendiary attack there will be realized as an extremely important by-product permanent fire damage to war plants located in or near the urban centers." (Kerr, p.19).

With respect to the new NDRC bomb developed by Bush and his team, the British suggested that "the oil bomb should supplant the magnesium bomb. The British L.C. 30-lb oil bomb per ton of bomb lift is some one to one and a half times as effective as the British or American 4-lb magnesium bomb for attacking German areas…The new U.S. 6.2-lb oil bomb is, the NDRC group believes, several times as effective as the 4-lb magnesium bomb on the same type of target." (Kerr, p.19)

Chapter 2: Bombing Missions in 1944

While American military officials were focused on bombing missions in Germany in 1942, that focus switched to Japan a year later as President Franklin D. Roosevelt and General George C. Marshall began analyzing potential bomber bases from which to launch missions against the Japanese home islands. Attempting to create a list of the most important Japanese industrial and economic targets, Raymond Ewell sent a memorandum to high-ranking military officials advocating for the use of the M-69 incendiary bomb: "The only reason that we, as development people, need be concerned with this matter is that the General Staff probably does not realize the extraordinary potential destructiveness of this bomb on Japanese cities, which puts it almost in the class of the oft-mentioned "secret weapon," [most likely the atomic bomb] and they probably are not taking this weapon into account in their strategy and planning. Anyone familiar with the M-69 and with the construction and layout of Japanese cities can make a few calculations and soon reach a tentative conclusion that even as small amounts as 10 tons of M-69's would have the possibility of wiping out major portions of any of the large Japanese cities…However, there are not over 20 persons in the country who are sufficiently familiar with the M-69 to form any judgment in this connection and probably not a one of these persons even knows anyone in the strategy and planning circles of the General Staff. It would seem that steps should be taken to bring this weapon and its possibilities to the attention of the General Staff at once." (Kerr, p.24).

The bomber that would be used in a mission against the Japanese home island was the B-29, which had a range of 3,250 miles at 25,000 feet and could carry a 5,000 pound payload. While the B-29 was designed for high-altitude bombing missions, Col. Emmett O'Donnell, Jr. became convinced that it should be used in a different capacity. In a memorandum to the Army Air Forces (AAF) board, he wrote, "As a matter of fact, for use in the specific task of attacking Japanese cities from Chinese bases with incendiary bombs, I believe this airplane could be used with greater effect without any armament by dispatching them singly at night and bombing by radar…Considering the difficulty our P-51s experienced in pressing home attacks in daylight, I

believe that the Japs would be absolutely frustrated in successfully attacking them at night…
This single-airplane operation would have the additional advantage of allowing the ships to be
used to their absolute maximum range. Great difficulty is to be expected in flying large
formations for great distances. The cooling of the engines is a critical item, and wingmen and
rear elements are bound to experience mechanical difficulties due to excess throttling." (Kerr,
p.59).

O'Donnell, Jr.

For the Japanese, a major problem in the defense of the home islands was the fact that they
lacked a plane that was able to intercept a high-altitude bomber like the B-29. The planes the
Japanese military did possess were designed to operate at 16,000 feet, well below the 25,000 feet
of the B-29s, but three major aircraft would be used in the defense of the Japanese home islands:
the Ki-61 was a single-engine fighter that had two 20-mm guns and two 12.7-mm machine guns;
the Ki-44 was also a single-engine plane that had two 12.7-mm guns and two 7.7-mm machine

guns; and the Ki-45 was a twin-engine plane that had three machine guns and a 37-mm cannon.

The defense of the home islands fell to three military groups. Tokyo was to be defended by the Eastern Army Command's 10th Air Division (400 planes), the rest of the island of Honshu would be defended by the Central Command's 11th Air Division (200 planes), and the western end of Honshu and the island of Kyushu would be defended by the Western Army Command's 12th Air Division (150 planes).

Along with fighter planes, the Japanese defense would also utilize anti-aircraft batteries that were mainly deployed around industrial cities like Tokyo, Yokohama, and Nagoya. However, the only antiaircraft gun that the Japanese possessed that was capable of reaching the B-29s at high altitude was their 120-mm model, and the production of that gun was limited. Moreover, at 21 tons, it was not a mobile weapon. As if that wasn't bad enough, Japanese radar systems were not as highly developed as the German systems in Europe, so the small number of radar units that were available were used around Tokyo and other major cities. For the rest of the home islands, sound-locating devices were used.

By 1944, interest in incendiary bombing missions on Japan increased, and in June of that year, the Committee of Operations Analysts created a subcommittee to study "the question of fire attacks upon urban industrial areas of Japan." (Kerr, p.71). Their findings were summarized in a report which stated, "In Tokyo, Osaka, and Nagoya between 15 and 20 percent of all manufacturing workers are employed in establishments so small in size that they can hardly be distinguished from dwelling units. These workshops are probably located in quite random fashion through the business, industrial and residential areas. Destruction of residential areas by fire would probably account for many small-scale manufacturing enterprises. Small-scale units very often serve as feeder plants and parts manufacturers to large factories. There is considerable evidence that small-scale units are producing parts for airplanes, machinery, ordnance items and other war material. Designs, technical advice, credit and equipment are frequently provided by the larger prime contractors…" (Kerr, p.72-73).

A simulation by the AAF of a bombing mission on Kobe, Japan, from the Marianas Islands produced some important results for subsequent operations. By simulating a high-altitude attack in broad daylight, the AAF calculated that 20% of the aircraft would fail to reach the target, and among those that did reach the target, an estimated 15-25% would miss. Based on this simulation, the AAF estimated that 153 B-29s would need to be deployed in order to destroy the city, and the AAF also estimated that night bombing or "blind" bombing during daylight hours would require twice as many bombers to accomplish the task.

In response to these findings, supporters of low-altitude incendiary bombing again noted the differences between past bombing missions and the situation in Japan. They noted that Japanese cities had higher population densities than German cities, and that buildings in Japan were also more flammable. Furthermore, they noted that the weather over Japan would be a hindrance to high-altitude precision bombing.

In the fall of 1944, American military personnel began building airstrips on the island of Saipan, one of the Mariana Islands. From Saipan, B-29s would be in range of the Japanese home islands, and the initial mission against Tokyo, dubbed "San Antonio I," would be a daytime precision bombing mission. General George Kenney was vocal in his criticism of the planned mission, as he believed most of the B-29s that would be launched for the mission would fail to reach Tokyo and that those that reached their targets would suffer heavy casualties.

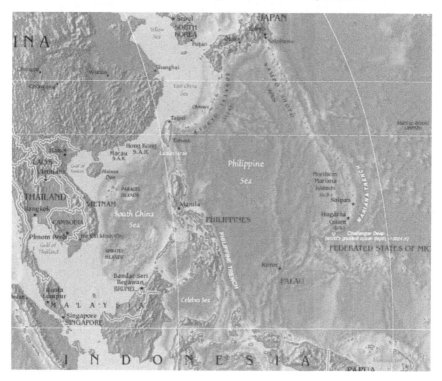

A map with Saipan in the center-right and the Japanese home islands at the top

Kenney

Despite Kenney's objections, the mission went forward, and on November 23, 1944, 111 B-29s took off from the runways of Saipan and flew toward the Japanese home islands. As the bombers reached the coast of Japan, they were confronted by Japanese planes and antiaircraft fire, and the ones that made it through had to deal with tailwinds reaching 140 mph, which gave the bombers groundspeeds of approximately 445 mph. This created problems for the bombardiers who were trying to accurately drop their payloads, and in all, only 24 B-29s dropped their bombs on the correct target zone. The other 64 B-29s that reached the designated areas dropped their bombs either on the dock areas of Tokyo or into Tokyo Bay.

Unbeknownst to them at the time, the B-29s had located the "jet stream," a band of air running from northern Siberia and across Japan that reached speeds of up to 500 mph at altitudes between 30,000-40,000 feet. Up until that time, nobody had much reason to worry about the jet stream because it was at such high altitudes, but it adversely affected the ability of American bombers to conduct high-altitude precision bombing runs.

Further attacks on the Japanese home islands, as well as Japanese-held territories like Singapore and Rangoon, met with mixed results, and it became increasingly clear that while the B-29 bombers were meeting expectations in terms of high-altitude bombing, the percentage of bombs hitting their targets and the amount of damage to those targets were proving inconsistent. In a letter to Air Force General Lauris Norstad, Arnold wrote, "I am still worried – we have built up ideas in the Army, the Navy, and among civilians of what we can do with our B-29s. We had all realized that in order to do considerable damage, large numbers of B-29s would have to deliver their loads of bombs against Japan continuously and consistently, and yet in spite of the above, really and truly, our average daily delivery rate against Japan is very, very small...Unless something drastic is done to change this condition soon, it will not be long before the B-29 is just another tactical airplane." (Kerr, p.123).

Norstad

Chapter 3: January-February 1945

Given the results of the initial raids, General LeMay began to move away from high-altitude bombing runs because of the frequency with which they missed their target. For example, 8 attacks against the Musashimo Tama plant had all failed due to a variety of reasons (the last failure being the result of bad weather causing sight problems for the bombers). In analyzing the previous bombing missions, Lieutenant Colonel Robert S. McNamara believed that radar bombing had not improved but that visual bombing had become a bit more accurate. He believed this increased accuracy was due to planes releasing their bombs at lower altitudes, and that the results became better with each 5,000 foot drop in elevation. LeMay also analyzed the bombing missions and felt that the Japanese were ramping up their defense of Tokyo and Nagoya.

McNamara

As a result, LeMay began ordering low-altitude night raids that would feature M-69 incendiary cluster bombs in an effort to destroy Japan's largest and most important cities. In a bombing run on January 23, 1945 over Tokyo, the 73rd Bomb Wing lost nine planes, which convinced LeMay to switch toward less heavily defended targets like Kobe and Nagoya. These missions also provided data on the use of incendiary bombs. As Norstad wrote to LeMay on February 12th, "We have run two test incendiary attacks [Nagoya and Kobe] the results of which have been inconclusive. It is absolutely necessary for us to know our capability with regard to incendiary attacks in the Japanese urban areas. We believe that the only diversion from the attack on the aircraft engine industry that is justifiable at this time is another major incendiary attack. It is recommended that the center of Zone I of Nagoya be used as the target. The immediate purpose of this attack is to produce a conflagration that is beyond the capacity of fire-fighting control." (Kerr, p.134).

On February 25th, LeMay returned his attention to Tokyo, authorizing a bombing mission that would use M-69 bombs. Due to poor weather conditions, the bombers would be authorized to bomb by radar, but since only one assembly point was created for three wings of bombers, the planes had massive problems as they circled around the designated area. Eventually, the aircraft "arrived over the target area individually or in small groups, at altitudes from 23,000 to 30,000 feet, from a variety of directions. The attack lasted over an hour and a half. One hundred and seventy airplanes dropped 411 tons of M-69 incendiaries through the clouds on a snow-blanketed Tokyo." (Kerr, p.141).

This time, Japanese defenses had a hard time targeting the bombers. No planes attempted to intercept the bombers, and Japanese anti-aircraft operators had problems targeting the bombers because they were not flying in large formations and came from different directions. Even with the problems of the single designated area, the attack was a huge success; more than 2,000 M-69 bomb clusters were dropped, and roughly one square mile of Tokyo was destroyed.

In conjunction with the changes in bombing strategies, American military officials began to change their stances on attacking civilian targets. In the middle of February 1945, the Allies were steadily advancing against the Germans from both east and west, with British and American forces having repulsed the German offensive during the Battle of the Bulge and the Soviet Union's Red Army pushing from the east. Indeed, the war would be over in just a little more than 2 months. Nonetheless, it was during this timeframe that the Allies conducted one of the most notorious attacks of the war: the targeting of Dresden. As a Royal Air Force memo put it before the attack, "Dresden, the seventh largest city in Germany and not much smaller than Manchester is also the largest unbombed builtup area the enemy has got. In the midst of winter with refugees pouring westward and troops to be rested, roofs are at a premium, not only to give shelter to workers, refugees, and troops alike, but to house the administrative services displaced from other areas. At one time well known for its china, Dresden has developed into an industrial city of first-class importance.... The intentions of the attack are to hit the enemy where he will feel it most, behind an already partially collapsed front... and incidentally to show the Russians when they arrive what Bomber Command can do."

In the span of about 48 hours, Dresden was targeted by over 1,200 Allied bombers, which dropped nearly 4,000 tons of explosives on the town. The firestorms caused by this pounding hollowed out 1,600 acres and killed at least tens of thousands in gruesome ways. Ironically, many of the victims in Dresden had fled from the eastern front as the Soviets advanced, understandably worried about what kind of punishment the Soviets would dole out to captured Germans in response to the atrocities committed in Russia during the war.

As the RAF memo noted, Dresden was relatively unscathed before the attacks, and the bombing was justified by the Allies based on Dresden being the home of hundreds of factories and a crucial railway. However, the widespread devastation immediately compelled the Nazis to use the attack as propaganda, and it has been condemned in the nearly 70 years since, with arguments still debating whether Dresden should've been attacked in the manner it was, and whether it was a disproportionate bombing. While most historians agree that the German war machine was in retreat by the time of this bombing of Germany's seventh largest city, other facts about the purpose and efficacy of the attack are less than decided. The debate over Dresden, which began shortly after the bombing and continues to this day, focuses not only on the necessity of the attack but also on the legitimacy of targets, and even on the disputed number of deaths that resulted.

Richard Peter's picture of the ruins of Dresden (part of the Deutsche Fotothek collection)

While the British had used a policy of attacking civilian targets in Germany, it was the first time Americans had deliberately done the same. As General Arnold put it after the firebombing of Dresden, "We must not get soft. War must be destructive and to a certain extent inhuman and ruthless." (Kerr, p. 145). Norstad and LeMay also supported this view for American operations over Japan, and it would color their approach in the coming months.

Chapter 4: March 1945

In early March 1945, LeMay made the decision to take a new approach to the bombing of Japan. The B-29 had been designed as a high-altitude precision bomber that was supposed to fly in large formations during daylight and conduct visual bombings. Now, however, they would be used at night, flying individually at altitudes between 7,000-8,000 feet and using radar to bomb targets. LeMay was especially driven by the belief that flying at low altitudes would allow his bombers to avoid the high winds and poor visibility that had consistently plagued previous bombing missions.

The bombers that would be featured in these raids were reconfigured specifically for low-altitude incendiary bombing. In order to lighten the load of the bombers so as to pack more bombs on board, the number of crew members was reduced. Bomber crews were also not equipped with machine guns because Japan only had two groups of fighter planes capable of defending the home islands at night. Even though subordinates argued against LeMay's decision to remove the machine guns, he stated, "I'm removing the ammunition because I'm afraid that the crews will be shooting at each other more than at Japs. Then, too, we'll save three thousand pounds, which will give us another ton and a half of bombs." (Hoyt, p. 2).

An additional issue was that American pilots had not been trained for night missions, but LeMay pushed on with his idea. LeMay noted, "It is my hope that night missions will reduce losses at sea, because returning B-29s will be over Iwo in daylight." LeMay was referring to Iwo Jima, which had recently been taken by American forces and provided a new landing site for bombers.

When the bomber crews were told of the plans and that the bombers would fly individually and without machine guns, many were shocked by how the missions went against standard protocol, but officers tried to raise morale by emphasizing how important the missions were and how they would destroy Japan's war-making capacity and morale.

During planning for this new kind of bombing raid, officials decided to target Tokyo. Specifically, they focused on Zone I, which was a densely populated area of about three miles which ran along the Sumida River. Zone I had six important targets that were on the 20th Air Force's target list, including the Hattori Company, whose factories made fuses for artillery shells. Other targets included railroad yards, stations, markets and storage facilities.

Zone I actually had few military targets relative to the other possible bombing areas, but Zone I included a mixed industrial, commercial, and residential area. Thus, it was heavily populated and would require the least number of incendiary bombs to destroy the area. Zone I also included many of the small plants that military officials believed were important to the Japanese war effort, and in terms of its residential areas, roughly 1.1 million people resided there. At 135,000 people per square mile, it was one of the most densely inhabited areas in the world, and many of the houses and barracks in Zone I were made of wood. They had been constructed in the aftermath of the Great Kanto Earthquake in 1923 to meet housing needs, but they had never been torn down after the area was built back up. In terms of the potential loss of human life, Ewell later stated, "You drop a load of bombs, and if you are cursed with any imagination at all, you have at least one quick horrid glimpse of a child lying in bed with a whole ton of masonry tumbling down on top of him, or a three-year-old girl wailing… Then you have to turn away from the picture if you intend to retain your sanity. And also if you intend to keep doing the work your nation expects of you." (Kerr, p.154).

On March 8th, LeMay announced "Meetinghouse #2" to the bomber squadrons. With the B-29 bombing campaign looking like it could not overcome the problems it had encountered in the bombing of the Japanese home islands, LeMay's new plan would help decide whether or not military commanders would continue the B-29 campaign or would call it off. 10 bomber groups would take part in the mission, and as intelligence officer Gould of the 9th Bomb Group noted, the instructions they were given included the following:

"A. Tokyo lies 25 mi. from mountains – 60 miles N.E. Fuji on coastal plain in the center of Honshu. As you can see from this relief of N. Honshu.

B. Your route carries you along the Chiba Peninsula to [word omitted in Gould's notes] and across on a heading of 304 to Iwaga Pt. at mouth of Goi River. You will be bombing at night & will probably see only L.W. Cont. [land-water contrast] & fires.

C. From Iwaga Point 15 miles – passing left of Chiba to center of Honjo Ward one mile East of Sumida River. Your target to right of arrowhead dock area – just to right of Sunamachi Airfield.

D. Tokyo bounded on south and west by TAMA – east and north by EDO. Don't be confused by 25' extension to south – 10 x 10

E. Honjo is west half of the area bounded by Sumida and Naka – 1500'. Honjo is 2 x 3 and Delta is 4 x 6

F. Elevation 183 feet.

G. Your radar Aiming Point is main R.R. bridge crossing Sumida at bulge to west – River here 400 feet. 3 bridges below – 7 above.

H. Your visual Aiming Point is 1 mile east of bridge across Sumida.

I. Remember all fires not ours.

J. P.O.W. – Several camps, some locations unknown – none known in target area.

V. Enemy Defenses

A. Flak and balloons covered by flak officer.

B. Many searchlights – wear red goggles.

C. No camouflage, dummies or smoke screens other than our own.

D. Give surface wind and velocity.

E. Experience recently over Empire most encouraging. Without trying to make you apprehensive, it is still our duty to tell you that there are, according to 21 Feb recon. 1. 60 twin 2. 300 single [fighters] 3. 80 airfields (13 combat fighter strips) others building 4. _____ night fighters 5. Keep lights out 73rd Wing jumped 200 miles out to sea.

F. Radar – you will be picked up but we hope enemy's sets will be confused and saturated.

VI. Caution [In case of capture]

A. Japanese money, souvenirs, diaries.
B. Name, rank and serial number only."

The reaction from the bomber crews ranged from acceptance (for more experienced crew members) to outrage. Some thought that LeMay was desperate and that they were about to suffer the consequences of it, but even with the mixed feelings about the mission, the members of the bomber crews knew that they had to undertake the mission.

As the bombers assembled and prepared for takeoff at roughly 7:00 p.m., Norstad sent a message to Washington: "Operations tonight will be largest yet, if plan can be carried out. Its effect may be significant. It over three hundred aircraft take off you should release that number. In any event release fact that largest number participated if that proves to be a fact. In order to establish foundation for what may be an outstanding show, you should leave no doubt that this is an important operation. We will give you further details as they may arise. Results are not certain until they can be seen so hold something back but it should be stressed that this is a big one." (Kerr, p. 166).

For LeMay, this was an important moment that he believed could change the course of the war:

"If this raid works the way I think it will, we can shorten the war. We've figured out a punch he's not expecting this time. I don't think he's got the right kind of flak to combat this kind of raid, and I don't think that he can keep his cities from being burned down – wiped right off the map." (Kerr, p.173).

The attack on the night of March 9-10 consisted of 324 B-29s carrying approximately 2,000 tons of firebombs. Flying in front of the bombers was a squadron of Pathfinders to provide targeting points for the bombs.

Japanese forces were first notified of the impending attack when the planes flew over Fushan Island at about 10:00 p.m. that night, but Japanese defenses were hampered. Winds that night reached as high as 80 miles per hour, disturbing radar and radio signals, and while radio stations on the home islands that were receiving reports of American bomber movements notified the navy, the army was not notified of the immanent attack. This delayed Japanese fighter squadrons from getting into the air to contest the skies. Furthermore, the Japanese defenses were surprised by how low the bombers were flying (at 10,000 feet rather than the 30,000 feet of previous bomber missions).

By tracking the movement of the incoming bombers, Japanese defense forces realized that the Americans were headed toward Tokyo, and that the attack would be centered in the Koto Basin, an industrial district that happened to be where 400,000 residents lived.

Nonetheless, there was only so much the Japanese could do at this stage of the war. During the raid, there was little anti-aircraft fire directed at the bombers, and in all only 14 B-29s were shot down and 42 others damaged by anti-aircraft fire. For those shot down, rescue teams were able to save 5 of the 14 crews shot down.

The lead bombers, upon reaching their destination point, dropped their M-47 bombs, creating fires and illuminating the area for the bombers following them. Bombers approached at different angles and from different directions, confusing anti-aircraft battery operators. It took roughly one hour for all bombers to drop their bombs on the area, which included a mix of M-47 and M-69 incendiaries.

Some of the bomber crews recalled the visual differences in the new low-altitude bombing; rather than seeing the outline of the entirety of the city, as occurred on clear days in high-altitude bombing runs, they could now make out buildings and streets illuminated by the fires that were spreading across the target areas. For example, the 29th Group's bombers had come in at 5,000 feet, while the 497th Group's bombers dropped their bombs at 7,500 feet. Jim Sherrell, of the *Southern Belle*, thought he could smell burning pine or cedar, two of the major types of wood used to construct many of the buildings in the city, even in the plane's cabin. Other bomber crews claimed they smelled burning flesh as they dropped their payloads in their designated areas.

General Power's B-29 was one of the bombers involved in the attack that night. After dropping their bombs, the B-29 climbed to 10,000 feet, where Power was able to survey the scene. He saw the small fires that had sprung up from the incendiary bombs they were dropping, and also how the wind pushed the fires together and increased their intensity. He also noted the lack of defense from the Japanese; few anti-aircraft batteries had fired on them, and even fewer planes had tried to intercept the bombers. Power circled Tokyo, watching the firestorm as it spread through the city, and he had some difficulty with the updrafts that were hitting his plane from the fires below. As the bomber left the area and returned to the Marianas, the tail gunner reported that he could still see the fires from 150 miles away.

Most civilians in Tokyo were asleep at 10:30 p.m. when the air raid warning sirens began to go off in the city. That provided precious little time for residents before the first B-29s were already releasing their bombs on the city, and while official proclamations about potential bombings stated that each family should stay and protect their houses by putting out fires that might occur there, most people tried to flee the situation because of the scale of the fires set off in Tokyo. As Toshiko Higashikawa, who was 12 years old at the time, recalled, "We hurried through the streets, joining the fleeing crowd. Buildings were burning everywhere. Father was wearing his big backpack. It was very scary and the hot wind from the fires burned our faces. When a plane came over very low, we all ducked and tried to hide ourselves. We could see the bombs coming out of the planes; sometimes they exploded in the street in front of us. There was fire everywhere. I saw one person caught by the claws of the fire dragon before you could say Jack Robinson! Her clothes just went up in flames. Another two people were caught, and burned up. The bombers just kept coming." (Hoyt, p.12).

In one tragic scene, citizens who had fled their homes sought shelter in a Buddhist temple dedicated to Kwan-Yin, Goddess of Mercy. The 200 year-old building was a place of safety for a brief period before it was ignited by the M-69s dropping nearby, but as those inside the building tried to exit, others were still trying to enter, causing a crush of people that left many people trampled in the panic.

Seizo Hashimoto was 13 years old at the time of the bombing, and he and his family lived in Koto ward, which was heavily hit by bombers. Hashimoto was separated from his family when the bombing began, and he remembered being terrified as the fire swept around him. He saw a woman, most likely a courtesan from the geisha district, caught in the fire. She was wearing a red kimono with gold and silver threads in her hair. She tried to run from the firestorm but was unable to outpace it, and as young Hashimoto watched her burn alive, a piece of her kimono was swept up by the wind and landed near his feet.

In Tokyo proper, bombers dropped bombs in 30 intervals from Tokyo Bay to Edo Gawa Ward, Koto Ward, Chuo Ward, Minato Ward, Oota Ward, Katsushika Ward, Kita Ward, Itabashi Ward, Shinjuku War, and then to Shibuya Ward in the west. It took roughly an hour for the bombers to drop their bombs, but because of the lack of defenses in the area, they were virtually untouched by anti-aircraft fire and fighters.

Since most Japanese houses were made of wood, they only intensified the raging fires. Near a Tokyo hostel, Masuko Harino remembered, "As the worry grew over the fate of the hostel, one of the young people, Yoshikawa-san, and I went toward the factory, as we all fled. Somehow we two got separated from the others as we ran away fearing death. People's clothes were on fire, a fiery drama it had become. Some people were writhing about in torment and no one had time to help them. In front of me I saw the Meiji theater filled with people, so many we could not get inside. Intense heat was coming from the firm storm. My eyes seemed about to pop out. Yoshikawa-san cut her way through the mob and I followed along the road, seeking some respite from the blowing heat of the terrible fire. We ran. We saw fleeing shapes, but little else. A telephone pole collapsed, and twisted electric wires snaked out along the ground. The road on both sides was full of people's possessions, burning up. My eyes hurt. Breathing was difficult and I felt that life was escaping me. I found a broken hydrant and soaked my *zukin* [air-raid turban] and put it on my head, almost unconsciously. Finally I fled as far as Kiyosu bridge..." (Edoin, p.68).

Tokyo's fire department was experienced in fighting fires associated with bombing runs, but they were unprepared for the destruction caused by the incendiary bombs. The firebombing destroyed many of the city's water mains, and the intense heat of the fires made it impossible to get to their center. Takeiro Ueba was a teenager who was also a member of the Young Volunteer Fireman's Association. As the bombing began, he helped his family to their designated safe area at a local park and then ran back to take up his duties as a firefighter. Ueba's situation was similar to firefighters across the city; the water mains in his area had failed, so he was forced to try to put out the fires with straw mats and sand.

In all, 96 fire engines were destroyed, while 88 firemen were killed in the bombing raid. Additionally, 500 civil guards also died, as these were men who worked with the fire department during emergency situations like the bombing raids.

Many of the people fleeing the fires tried to cross the Sumida River, hoping that the far banks would be a place of safety for them. Some residents, upon reaching river bank, decided to stay at Sumida Park, a large open park that seemed like it could provide safety from the fires. However, as the fires approached the park, the heat and flames compelled civilians toward the river's edge and into the water. Since it was March, the water was only about 40 degrees Fahrenheit, making it hard for people to stay in the river for long. Many of the people who went into the river to escape ended up drowning, while many of those who decided to remain in the park died of burns and asphyxiation.

One survivor recalled his harrowing experience in the river that night after he was forced to jump in when the fire reached the bridge: "I didn't have a life preserver so I had to swim again, but I had no energy left. And then I realized I touched something. It was a buoy that had floated down river from the equipment shop that was burning near Azuma Bridge. A very good idea hit me under the hellish conditions…I didn't know when my arms would give out, but if I could hold onto that buoy…" (Hoyt, p. 68).

He then undid his belt and used it to fasten himself to the buoy. "It was hard to breathe, but I managed, and then the dawn came and in my reflection in the water I saw I had blood all over my head. My face was burned and swollen. I felt a stinging pain in my face and neck, because of the dirt in the river. All I saw around me was dead bodies. I grew dizzy and I fainted away. When I regained consciousness, I was lying on the riverbank. I had been rescued by somebody near Umaya Bridge." (Hoyt, p. 68).

One of the major bridges spanning the river was the Kototoi Bridge, and thousands of people did not stop at Sumida Park but instead either crossed the bridge to the other side or remained on the bridge as a place of refuge. Unfortunately, the enclosed space of the bridge led to more scenes of trampling. The next morning, the survivors of the attack found that the bridge was filled with dead bodies, as was the river.

In Asakusa ward, many families sought shelter at the Futabe Grade School, which had a basement that had been designed as an air raid shelter. The building was also fireproof, and like other such buildings in the city, it was considered a good place to seek safety. Tragically, in many of these buildings, sparks and fire entered the buildings, most likely through windows shattered by the heat of the fires or through cracks in the walls, igniting the materials inside. These buildings then trapped the fire and heat within their walls, suffocating or burning those who had sought shelter within. At Futabe School, only those people who fled to the roof of the building managed to survive, and for Hidezo Tsuchikura, the sparks and flames that reached them even on the roof would have burned him and his family had it not been for a nearby water tank that they were able to get in to avoid their clothing being set on fire.

Sirens signaling the end of the air raid went off at 3:20 a.m., about 20 minutes after the last bomber of the 313th Bomb Wing had dropped its payload on the city. By 6:00 in the morning, fires were burning across central Tokyo (and some would burn for days before being put out), but for the most part, the death and destruction was over.

That day, March 10, the citizens and government officials of Tokyo had to deal with two major problems: disposing of the massive number of dead bodies in the city and providing food and shelter for the survivors of the bombing raid. The army, police, and fire department worked together to locate, identify, and dispose of the dead. Many of the dead were burned beyond recognition, while others had fled from their home districts and were now unknown to local officials. Most of the dead were unidentified and buried in pits in groups of 20 or more.

Captain Kubota was a member of the Army Command's Rescue Unit Number 1, one of the teams that tried to help survivors. Kubota and his team left at 3:50 a.m., about half an hour after the siren announced the end of the air raid, and as they drove through the streets, they could see the movement of the large fires in the city, as well as the destruction that it had brought. When they reached the Kudanshita army command post, volunteer women and children were there trying to find survivors amid the ruins of the city. A major problem that night was that the temperature had dropped to near-freezing. This made it difficult for both rescue workers and survivors as they tried to keep warm. Moreover, there was a lack of supplies; Kubota was told he would have to work without penicillin, an important antibiotic.

Adding to the carnage, telephone and electric lines had fallen into the streets, as had overhead lines from the rail lines. These were all potentially dangerous for people trying to move through the city. The streets were also littered with broken glass, pieces of metal, burned handcarts, wagons, and bicycles, as well as dead horses and human remains.

As Kubota's team crossed the Ryogoku Bridge and viewed the Ichido River, they were appalled to see a mass of dead bodies around the bridge. Across the Sumida River, they saw a similar scene. Bodies were burned beyond the point of recognition, and many were charred to the point that touching them caused them to disintegrate into ash.

In addition to the massive physical damage to the city, there was also the psychological blow that the bombing had caused. The Japanese had been told that Tokyo could never be bombed, so this kind of massive destruction was incomprehensible on one hand and completely demoralizing on the other. The survivors of the attack were taken to undamaged buildings, where they were sheltered from the elements. They were given food and blankets, but these were only available in limited supply. Many now-homeless residents of Tokyo were transported to the countryside, while others were taken to areas in the western part of the city that had avoided much of the destruction of the central districts, but even there, refugees had to be placed in large public buildings as accommodations were in short supply.

Japanese estimates in the aftermath of the attack stated that Asakusa, Honjo, Fukugawa, Joto, and Shitaya wards had been nearly completely destroyed in the bombings. 267,171 buildings had been burned, which amounted to roughly 25% of the buildings in the city. Furthermore, an estimated 83,793 people had died in the attack, while 40,918 had been injured. Over 1 million people were made homeless in the aftermath of the attack. While this was a devastating finding, equally devastating was the effect that the bombings had on Tokyo's production capabilities; in addition to factories that were destroyed, 25% of the industrial workforce in the city had been incapacitated.

Pictures taken in the wake of the March 9-10 raid

In the aftermath of the attack, the emperor insisted on going out into the city to see the damage that had been caused by the bombing raid. Imperial officials tried to convince him not to go, as they believed the scenes he would witness were too ghastly for his eyes, but Hirohito would not relent, and he forced his officials to send an Imperial caravan into the city. The emperor dressed in his military uniform for the occasion.

Hirohito first visited the banks of the Sumida River, which by this time had been cleared of the dead bodies that had packed the river and its banks. He spoke with some of the volunteers and survivors and then moved on to a refugee camp, where he again offered his condolences to those he saw. Word began to spread among Tokyo's residents that the emperor had come to view the damage and speak to survivors, and this deeply moved many of the refugees who had lost their homes, possessions, and loved ones in the attack.

Pictures of Hirohito surveying the ruins

Although Hirohito personally believed that this had been an attack from which Japan could not recover, his military officials continued their policy of putting on a brave face and emphasizing their nation's power and resilience. Japan publicly acknowledged the attack in a war communiqué from Imperial Headquarters on March 10th: "Today, approximately 130 B-29s, with their main force, raided Tokyo from a little after midnight to 0240 and carried out blind bombing attacks on certain sections. Resulting from this blind bombing attack, various places within the city were set afire. However, fire in the Shime-Ryo of the Imperial Household Ministry was put out at 0235 and others were all extinguished around 0800. The war results thus far confirmed are as follows: 15 planes shot down and about 50 planes damaged." (Kerr, p. 210).

While this report tried to minimize the impact of the bombings, Japanese officials eventually had to acknowledge the large-scale destruction that they had suffered in their capital city. The Japanese government later released information regarding the scale of damage they had suffered. As Tokyo radio reported, "The man [LeMay] who invented and carried out the big raids of Hamburg now directs the attacks on Japan from the Marianas. A few nights ago he repeated here in Tokyo what he had learned in Germany. Owing to various unfavorable circumstances the storm of fire caused by incendiaries swept whole districts, which were burned to the ground;

only here and there were blackened walls of the rare stone building left standing. That bright, starlit night will remain in the memory of all who witnessed it…"

In an attempt to increase morale among Japanese civilians, Emperor Hirohito highlighted the exploits of Japanese fighter pilots. One of these was Lieutenant Heikichi Yoshizawa: "Lieutenant Yoshizawa, who shot down two B-29s and damaged four others in a series of B-29 raids on Tokyo, also damaged another enemy bomber over Shimodate when the B-29s attacked the Kanto district on February 10 this year. Although his plane was damaged by enemy gunfire he deliberately launched a ramming attack on another enemy plane and downed it, thereby meeting glorious death." (Edoin, p.5).

The Japanese media also tried to play down the attacks. As one newspaper wrote, "The other day, when I was about to get aboard a homebound electric car, I met a jovial friend of mine whom I had not seen for a long time. After the exchange of usual greetings the conversation naturally veered to air raids. At the end my jovial friend, to the accompaniment of a hearty guffaw said, 'Well, we sure are going to *endenizen* [make citizens of] these American fliers, don't you think? I said nothing, but I too laughed heartily. Believe it or not, the air raid has aroused in us a feeling of cheerfulness, a kind of lighthearted buoyance such as we experience when something long expected happens." (Edoin, p.227).

Nevertheless, other articles were more serious about the effects of the bombing raids:

"The women of Tokyo are exhibiting their bravery, particularly in the form of firefighting that is the most important function of the civil air-raid defense. Clad in *monpei*, with buckets in their hands, young women, together with men with their trousers wrapped in puttees and armed with firefighting implements, put out fires at the risk of their lives. When in one district a Buddhist temple was hit by an incendiary bomb, it was found extremely difficult to climb onto the roof, which was in flames. Yet the men and women firefighters, clasping their buckets and other implements in their teeth, ascended the roof and stamped out the blaze in no time. I was much struck with the smiling face of a little girl whose house was damaged by the concussion of a bomb falling nearby and who related to me quite calmly and composedly her experience right after the dropping of the bomb. It is impossible to forget her beaming face." (Edoin, p.228).

"United States Army Air Forces attacks on Tokyo are known among Japanese as 'blind' bombing or 'indiscriminate' air raids because nonmilitary business and residential districts have been targets of these attacks, while noncombatant civilians have been ruthlessly victimized. 'Blind' bombing or 'indiscriminate' – these expressions have appeared in our official communiqués but are now regarded as a gross misnomer in describing the enemy's savage attacks. It is now thought more appropriate to call them 'slaughter' bombing, a natural reflection of the growing popular indignation against their brutal bombing attacks." (Kerr, p.211).

The chief of the National Police Agency even went so far as to suggest in an interview that the effect of further bombing raids could be lessened through experience: "It is doubtless true that our houses of wood and paper, as foreigners term them, are at a disadvantage in air raids. But with training and courage, why should they be feared? Fire, wherever it originates, will always run up the paper walls to the ceiling. Provided it is then prevented from going higher by a partition of earth, tin, or even of wood, above the ceiling, it can then be checked there with water. If, however, it brings the ceiling down and gets onto the roof, it will at once spread everywhere and the whole building will be enveloped in flames." (Hoyt, p. 57)

Authorities began telling citizens that they needed to remove all flammable objects from their homes, and that when the air-raid sirens began to sound, they should take down their *shoji*, which were screens separating the rooms of the house. If there was not enough time to take down the *shoji*, they should smash them, along with other combustibles, so that they would not provide fuel for the fires. If and when the fires began, the authorities told residents that the best way to put them out was to smother it with mats, but if the fire had progressed, then they should use buckets of water. In order to put out the fires efficiently, the authorities told residents that neighbors should work together to pass buckets of water until the fire engines arrived. Taking these precautions, they told city residents that only one in three families would be affected by the next incendiary bombing raid.

Perhaps not surprisingly, despite the official propaganda coming from Japan's military and civil authorities, residents began to question much of what they were being told. In the aftermath of the Tokyo bombing, vocal criticism of the military could be heard for one of the first times as people questioned why the Japanese air force did not intercept American bombers as they began their raids. Japanese civilians also wondered why the government had not provided public air raid shelters for residents like other nations had done. As the government failed to respond to these criticisms, people began to take the position not just that Japan could not win the war but that Japan might be destroyed as a consequence of the war. One of the major promises of General Tojo, who had been Japan's prime minister until the fall of Saipan, was that Japan would never be bombed. This now turned out to be a false promise.

As word spread about the nature of the firebombing of Tokyo, *The New York Times'* Sunday edition on March 11th reported, "SPECIAL FIRE BOMB USED TO SET BLAZES IN JAPAN...Why flames spread so fast and leaped so high in Tokyo on Saturday was made clear today when the Army's Chemical Warfare Service released a limited description of the M-69 incendiary bomb, designed especially for use in Japan. At about 5,000 feet the 500-pound cluster bomb opens, releasing individual six-pound bombs filled with jellied gasoline. Each small bomb spreads burning gasoline for some thirty yards around upon exploding." (Kerr, p.213).

As the report in the *Times* indicated, few people in the United States discussed the death toll caused by the bombing. However, some were deeply disturbed, including J. Robert Oppenheimer, the director of the Manhattan Project. Although Oppenheimer's work was instrumental in the use of atomic bombs on Hiroshima and Nagasaki a few months later, he stated that he "thought it appalling that there should be no protest in the United States over such wholesale slaughter." Similarly, according to one of his friends, Vannevar Bush seemed to have been affected by the civilian death toll: "For years after the war Van Bush would wake up screaming in the night because he burned Tokyo. Even the atomic bomb didn't bother him as much as jellied gasoline." (Kerr, p.214).

Chapter 5: Subsequent Bombing Missions

After the success of the incendiary bombing of Tokyo, LeMay switched his focus to Japan's other major cities. American bombers used the new strategy in attacks on Nagoya, Osaka, and Kobe, each of which was hit a day apart in what LeMay called an "air blitz." In Nagoya, firefighters were better equipped to handle the fires than those in Tokyo, so the bombing mission there only destroyed two square miles. In Nagoya, however, LeMay fully understood Japan's lack of defensive resources when no bombers were shot down in the attack, and from that point on, he realized that he could bomb Japan virtually unopposed. At Osaka, LeMay continued to refine his strategy of low-altitude bombing, and the plan was honed into one in which the goal was to "get as many airplanes over the target as you can in the least amount of time and release your incendiaries so as to achieve maximum density of ground bursts." (Kerr, p.217). At Osaka, 8.1 square miles of the city were destroyed, along with 130,000 houses and roughly 4,000 civilians killed. At Kobe, as at Nagoya, the relative amount of damage was limited, as only 2.9 square miles of the city were destroyed, but 2,600 were killed and 65,000 houses were destroyed.

In the aftermath of this series of attacks, *Newsweek* ran an article titled "JAPAN: IN PANIC," reporting, "No Jap – and for that matter few Americans – had ever expected that such attacks could be mounted…the vital centers of four of Japan's five greatest cities burned out…an entirely new technique of bombing for the Army Air Forces…The top planning had been done in Washington under Brigadier General Lauris O. Norstad…the details were left to Major General Curtis E. LeMay." (Kerr, p.219)

LeMay also received a letter from General Arnold congratulating him on the new bombing tactics: "A study of the effect of the Tokyo attack of March 10 and the knowledge that by July 1 you will have nearly a thousand B-29s under your control leads one to conclusions that are impressive even to old hands at bombardment operations. Under reasonably favorable conditions you should be able to destroy whole industrial cities should that be required." (Kerr, p.220)

One of the unintended consequences of the blitz was that LeMay had depleted his stock of incendiary bombs. The Army Air Force had dropped over 9,000 tons of incendiary bombs, and they did not have a large enough reserve to continue large-scale firebombing. LeMay asked for an emergency shipment of 36,000 tons of M-47s and M-69s, and this request was quickly agreed to, but transporting the weaponry across the Pacific would take weeks before reaching their destination.

By April 13th, LeMay had bolstered his stock of incendiaries enough so that he could return to his bombing missions. That day, 327 B-29s struck Tokyo, this time in the northwest section of the city, where 2,124 tons of bombs destroyed 11.4 square miles of the city. On the 15th, Tokyo was hit again, with 303 B-29s destroying 6 square miles of the city, along with 3.6 miles in neighboring Kawasaki.

At this point, LeMay had again used up his stock of incendiaries, and with a need to support the American invasion of Okinawa, he had to again move away from his campaign of incendiary bombing. But even as the focus switched to Okinawa, LeMay still kept an eye on what he believed was his larger mission. In a letter to Norstad in late April, he wrote, "I am influenced by the conviction that the present stage of development of the air war against Japan presents the Army Air Forces for the first time with the opportunity of proving the power of the strategic air arm. I consider that for the first time strategic air bombardment faces a situation in which the strength is proportionate to the magnitude of the task. I feel that the destruction of Japan's ability to wage war lies within the capability of this command, provided its maximum capacity is exerted unstintingly during the next six months, which is considered to be the critical period. Though natural reluctant to drive my force at an exorbitant rate, I believe that the opportunity now at hand warrants extraordinary measures on the part of all sharing it." (Kerr, p.229).

LeMay's position was supported by military officials in Washington, who believed, "The effect on the morale of the Japanese people of the burning of their major cities with the destruction wrought therein and casualties caused cannot be evaluated statistically but the possibility exists that this alone might break the will of the people to continue to fight. This may be the thing that will bring home the futility of continuing the war to the Japanese people as well as the leaders of Japan. The Japanese industrialists must recognize that recuperation [of a destroyed industrial base] will take many, many years after the war and that they must depend on their industry to be a national power in peacetime…Incendiary attacks on Japanese inflammable Zone I areas of her major cities have been disastrous for the Japanese. It is believed that no other form of attack can bring home so clearly to the Japanese people the power of the Air Forces to destroy Japan as an industrial nation." (Kerr, p.230)

In early May, Germany announced its surrender, and at that point, Admiral Nimitz released LeMay's bomber group from its support role in Okinawa because he anticipated a troop surge as personnel and material moved from Europe to Asia. LeMay therefore returned to his incendiary campaign. On May 14th, he hit Nagoya again, with two raids destroying 7 square miles of the city.

After attacking Nagoya, LeMay returned his attention to Tokyo. In the previous attacks on Tokyo, American bombers had destroyed 34.2 square miles of the city, so the targets this time were areas south of the Imperial Palace, as well as the west side of Tokyo Bay. These areas were less populated than those previously attacked, but they did contain important strategic targets, such as aircraft and tank manufacturing plants, petroleum refineries, and railroad car plants.

During previous attacks, bombers had come into the city from the west, so this time LeMay planned for them to fly in from the east. By this time, Japanese military officials had tweaked their defense plans for Tokyo; in addition to being more experienced in firing at low-altitude bombers, the military had moved rocket batteries into position to defend the city. Moreover, instead of merely using searchlights to illuminate enemy bombers, they now also had flare batteries which could light up sections of the sky for anti-aircraft operators to shoot down planes. In addition to that, Japan had started to implement the "Baka," which was modeled on the kamikaze pilots who crashed into naval vessels. Baka were "small, rocket-propelled airplane[s]" carried in medium-range bombers. When enemy bombers attacked, the Baka would be released, and their pilots tried to crash them into the oncoming B-29s. The name "Baka" actually came from Americans, who named the suicide planes after the Japanese term for "fool."

Pictures of Baka planes

After this mission against Tokyo, which was conducted on May 25, bomber crews reported details about these new defensive measures. They noted that the Japanese were using new searchlights, which included some with beams that were five feet in diameter. While those swept the skies, others were used to illuminate single bombers. The flares were also new to the Americans; some were attached to parachutes that hung in the sky above the bombers, while others burst and lit up an area for a brief period before going out. The rocket batteries seemed to have been ineffective since most missed their targets, but their addition to the crowded skies increased the tense atmosphere among the bomber crews.

Thanks to some of the defense measures, the May 25 mission over Tokyo was one of the costliest for American bombers, as 26 B-29s were shot down. Along with the bombers that were shot down, 100 of the 464 bombers taking part in the mission were damaged by anti-aircraft fire. One observer from the 504th Bomb Group described witnessing planes going down:

"11:40 P.M. Over the target, on fire in a dive, blew up on ground

12:07 A.M. Seen to blow up 20 miles from coast on route out

1:07 A.M. On east edge of target, on fire for 5 minutes. No parachutes seen

1:20 A.M. Two miles from the coast on route out. Blew up, 5 chutes observed, probably 2 or 3 more

1:32 A.M. Small, flickering engine fire for two minutes. Was getting tracer fire from what seemed to be a turret – possibly a B-29. Blew up. [Over-anxious gunners in a B-29 may have thought the flame from the burning engine looked like a Baka]

1:35 A.M. Five miles south of Choshi Point and on fire. Blew up. No chutes seen." (Kerr, p.246).

An American POW, Sgt. Walter Odlin, was being held in Tokyo at the time of the bombing, and he recalled the raid: "The tiny planes [Bakas?] flew against the bombers and exploded, shattering into a thousand pieces. The bombers both burst into flame but remained intact while they came slowly down and crashed. The bombers hit by antiaircraft shells and by fire from Zeros likewise caught on fire, but in a score of instances their crews managed to extinguish the flames and keep on flying." (Kerr, p.250). Other American POWs were being held in a prison complex in Tokyo that burned down in the bombing. 62 of them died.

This second major firebombing of Tokyo hit the Imperial Palace, even though the area had been declared an "open city" and the government had given instructions that it was not to be bombed. "Almost all bombardiers excepted the Imperial Palace aiming point but in the night bombing they failed to verify accuracy and so the palace, segregated from the government by its distinctive wide moat, was bombed by at least one plane." (Hoyt, p. 96). The emperor and empress, along with the imperial household, were unharmed in the attack because an air-raid shelter had been built on the grounds in 1941. This shelter was three stories deep, with a ground floor for the imperial family, a service level with air conditioning and ventilation, and a deep shelter with servants quarters and a large meeting room. Emperor Hirohito and his family had moved into the shelter in 1943 after the war had turned against Japan.

Meanwhile, Hiroshi Shimamura, minister of State, was brought into an air-raid shelter at the home of Kantaro Suzuki, the prime minister. As the bombing began, the prime minister's house was hit, and smoke began to enter the shelter. As the people inside evacuated, they saw pillars of smoke coming from the direction of the Imperial Palace. According to Shimamura, "This scene was beyond description." (Hoyt, p.97).

Since the May 25 mission hit new areas of Tokyo that had previously been relatively untouched, many of the city's historic buildings were hit during this raid, including the Denzuin Temple in Koishikawa. Kazuko Ochi lived near the temple, and even though much of Tokyo had been destroyed in previous bombing missions, this was Ochi's first experience with the bombing campaign. Ochi was relatively lucky in that the apartment building had a bomb shelter in the garden area. According to Ochi, one of the men who entered the shelter had previously experienced three bombing raids, and he quickly decided that the shelter was not the best place to be, so he left.

While the bomb shelter provided protection, Ochi found that the air inside the shelter "was so bad and it got so hot inside the shelter that I was afraid that all of us would be roasted." Thus, Ochi ended up leaving the shelter and climbed a hill leading up to the Red Gate of Tokyo University. Ochi ended up staying with a friend for the remainder of the night, and upon going back to the apartment building the next day, Ochi was amazed to discover that the building was one of the only buildings in that area that had not been destroyed.

The firebombing of Tokyo on May 25 would be the last one targeting the city. In the wake of this raid, LeMay and his advisors estimated that 16.8 square miles of the city were destroyed, a larger total than any of the previous missions. In total, the six incendiary bombing missions against the Japanese capital had destroyed 56.3 square miles, or roughly half of the city, and all of the designated targets in the city had been destroyed, so Tokyo was taken off the list of urban incendiary bombing targets.

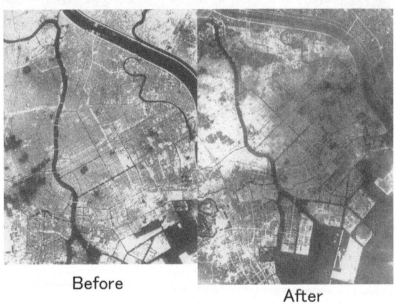

Before

After

Pictures taken in the wake of the firebombing on May 25

Chapter 6: The Aftermath

Even in late April 1945, Japan's military authorities still spoke of a decisive battle that they believed would occur when American soldiers tried to invade the home islands. Thus, they refused to surrender, even as more and more civilians wanted the war to end. As a result, many Japanese soldiers who had served in the war and had been discharged were redrafted for the coming battle. One man who was redrafted summed up the feelings of many Japanese citizens:

> "Every time we had an air raid, we lost not only human lives but buildings, enterprises, and industries. We were forced to shut down. Lack of materials, nonfunctioning production in limbo, this must happen to publishing, banking, industry, merchants, farmers. There is no exception.

> "After I enlisted in the army this second time, I was living in a lodge on the Pacific ocean in Kochi Province, on the island of Shikoku…Here we soldiers didn't have any drills. We were told we were waiting for the 'decisive battle' that our superiors had promised us to stop the Americans from landing on the sacred soil of Japan…

> "We were to fight to the last man, but we did not have anything with which to fight. The Japanese Army at home did not have any weapons. The Army didn't have any uniforms to spare; not even shoes; so we wore *waraji* – sandals made of straw. A soldier had to be able to make his own *waraji*. If he didn't have any skills he had to go barefoot." (Hoyt, p. 108).

Although the bombing campaign against Tokyo and the other major cities of Japan had taken a huge toll on the civilian population, Japanese military leaders continued to believe that they would fight until the end against the Americans. Indeed, it was not until a different kind of bomb was used on Japan a few months later that Hirohito decided to surrender.

Ironically, the atomic bombs that finally compelled Japan to surrender were used in large measure due to the fanatic resistance the Japanese had previously put up in 1945. Near the end of 1944, as Allied forces were pushing across the Pacific and edging ever closer to Japan, plans were drawn up to invade the Ryuku islands, the most prominent of them being Okinawa. Military planners anticipated that an amphibious campaign would last a week, but instead of facing 60,000 Japanese defenders as estimated, there were closer to 120,000 on the island at the beginning of the campaign in April 1945. The Battle of Okinawa was the largest amphibious operation in the Pacific theater, and it would last nearly 3 months and wind up being the fiercest in the Pacific theater during the war, with nearly 60,000 American casualties and over 100,000 Japanese soldiers killed. In addition, the battle resulted in an estimated 40,000-150,000 Japanese civilian casualties.

Okinawa witnessed every conceivable horror of war both on land and at sea. American ground forces on Okinawa had to deal with bad weather (including a typhoon), anti-tank moats, barbed wire, mines, caves, underground tunnel networks, and fanatical Japanese soldiers who were willing to use human shields while fighting to the death. Allied naval forces supporting the amphibious invasion had to contend with Japan's notorious kamikazes, suicide pilots who terrorized sailors as they frantically tried to shoot down the Japanese planes before they could hit Allied ships. As *The Marine Corps Gazette* noted, "More mental health issues arose from the Battle of Okinawa than any other battle in the Pacific during World War II. The constant bombardment from artillery and mortars coupled with the high casualty rates led to a great deal of men coming down with combat fatigue. Additionally the rains caused mud that prevented tanks from moving and tracks from pulling out the dead, forcing Marines (who pride themselves on burying their dead in a proper and honorable manner) to leave their comrades where they lay. This, coupled with thousands of bodies both friend and foe littering the entire island, created a scent you could nearly taste. Morale was dangerously low by the month of May and the state of discipline on a moral basis had a new low barometer for acceptable behavior. The ruthless atrocities by the Japanese throughout the war had already brought on an altered behavior (deemed so by traditional standards) by many Americans resulting in the desecration of Japanese remains, but the Japanese tactic of using the Okinawan people as human shields brought about a new aspect of terror and torment to the psychological capacity of the Americans."

Given the horrific nature of the combat, and the fact that it was incessant for several weeks, it's no surprise that Okinawa had a profound psychological effect on the men who fought, but it also greatly influenced the thinking of military leaders who were planning subsequent campaigns, including a potential invasion of the Japanese mainland. Most importantly, the Battle of Okinawa was so ruthless that it convinced Allied leaders that the invasion of Japan would be an absolute bloodbath for all sides. American military officials estimated that there would be upwards of a million Allied casualties if they had to invade the Japanese mainland, and if they were successful, Japan would suffer tens of millions of casualties in the process. As the Battle of Okinawa was about to finish, America's secret Manhattan Project was on the brink of its final goal: a successful detonation of a nuclear device. On July 16, 1945, the first detonation of a nuclear device took place in Alamogordo, New Mexico.

Before making his decision to use the bomb, President Harry Truman considered some of the ethical advice submitted by American physicists, particularly the idea of warning the Japanese to surrender before using a nuclear weapon. At the Potsdam Conference on July 26th, the U.S., the United Kingdom and China issued the Potsdam Declaration, giving the Japanese an ultimatum to surrender or suffer "prompt and utter destruction."

Japan chose to ignore the ultimatum, and ultimately Truman chose to use the bombs. Truman took ethical concerns into account, but the deadly experience of Okinawa made clear that hundreds of thousands of Americans would be casualties in a conventional invasion of the mainland of Japan. Moreover, the fanatical manner in which Japanese soldiers and civilians held out on Okinawa indicated that the Japanese would suffer more casualties during an invasion than they would if the bombs were used. Thus, pursuant to the Quebec Agreement, Canada and Great Britain consented to the use of the bomb, and as a result, Truman authorized its use on two sites in Japan.

The atomic bombings of Hiroshima and Nagasaki in August 1945 also remain controversial, but one of the most telling facts about the events that ended the war in the Pacific is that more Japanese died at Okinawa than in both atomic bombings combined. The firebombing of Tokyo on March 9-10 had also produced more casualties than either atomic bomb.

Emperor Hirohito addressed his Cabinet on August 14th, and in his speech, he told them, "It is my desire that you, my ministers of state, accede to my wishes and forthwith accept the Allied reply." The Cabinet's reply to Hirohito's speech was to unanimously accept his wishes. As General Anami, the leading opponent of surrender, stated, "As a Japanese soldier I must obey my emperor." The next day, Hirohito addressed the Japanese public and explained to them that Japan "must bear the unbearable." Of course, few civilians considered surrender unbearable by this point; upon hearing of the Emperor's surrender ending World War II, Takako Iga admitted, "When we heard the Emperor's words, speaking of the surrender of Japan, we could only thank God. It meant that from that point on we could go to bed at night and be sure we would be alive when morning came." (Edoin, p.239).

When American occupation forces came ashore to take control of Japan in the aftermath of World War II, they were shocked by what they saw. Marine Sergeant Joe O'Donnell was a combat photographer who documented what he saw of postwar Japan. He took photographs of "an old man dying of radiation burns after the Nagasaki atom bomb, hungry and homeless children, ragged families with nothing but the clothes on their backs, the utter wretchedness of a society destroyed." O'Donnell locked these photographs in a trunk, too disturbed to do anything with them, and a full 50 years would pass before he published the photographs documenting the destructive results of the American bombing campaigns. In all, the firebombing of Tokyo killed 200,000 people by official estimates (more than the 112,000 people killed by the atomic bombs), and given the lack of precise estimates (especially in the wake of the March 10-11 bombing raid), the number of Japanese deaths could have been as high as 300,000 people.

For his part, LeMay believed that his firebombing campaign had won the war against Japan. While that conclusion is up for debate among historians, the psychological effects of the campaign cannot be disputed. LeMay believed he had accomplished the goal of forcing Japan into a quicker surrender than would have happened otherwise, but for some civilians, the bombing campaign had created the opposite effect: since they believed they were going to die anyway, many were compelled to fight to the death against an American invasion force.

LeMay's campaign almost certainly reduced American casualties by helping ensure the military never had to undertake an invasion of the Japanese home islands, but that wasn't much of a consolation to the Japanese, who considered him responsible for the deaths of hundreds of thousands of Japanese citizens. In the wake of World War II, he was known colloquially as "Devil LeMay" in Japan.

Ironically, in 1964, nearly 20 years after he reduced Tokyo to rubble, LeMay was given the First Class Order of the Grand Cordon of the Rising Sun, the highest honor that the Japanese government could give a foreigner. Of course, this was made possible by the fact that America had reconstructed Japan during the postwar occupation and transformed it into a Cold War ally, but it was undoubtedly ironic for the surviving Japanese who had managed to live through the firebombing of Japan's capital.

Online Resources

Other World War II titles by Charles River Editors

Bibliography

Caidin, Martin (1960). A Torch to the Enemy: The Fire Raid on Tokyo. Balantine Books. ISBN 0-553-29926-3. D767.25.T6 C35.

Coffey, Thomas M. (1987). Iron Eagle: The Turbulent Life of General Curtis LeMay. Random House Value Publishing. ISBN 0-517-55188-8.

Frank, Richard B. (2001). Downfall: The End of the Imperial Japanese Empire. Penguin. ISBN 0-14-100146-1.

Grayling, A. C. (2007). Among the Dead Cities: The History and Moral Legacy of the WWII Bombing of Civilians in Germany and Japan. New York: Walker Publishing Company Inc. ISBN 0-8027-1565-6.

Greer, Ron (2005). Fire from the Sky: A Diary Over Japan. Jacksonville, Arkansas, U.S.A.: Greer Publishing. ISBN 0-9768712-0-3.

Guillian, Robert (1982). I Saw Tokyo Burning: An Eyewitness Narrative from Pearl Harbor to Hiroshima. Jove Pubns. ISBN 0-86721-223-3.

Hoyt, Edwin P. (2000). Inferno: The Fire Bombing of Japan, March 9 – August 15, 1945. Madison Books. ISBN 1-56833-149-5.

Jablonski, Edward (1971). "Air War Against Japan". Airwar Outraged Skies/Wings of Fire. An Illustrated history of Air power in the Second World War. Doubleday. ASIN B000NGPMSQ.

Lemay, Curtis E.; Bill Yenne (1988). Superfortress: The Story of the B-29 and American Air

Power. McGraw-Hill Companies. ISBN 0-07-037164-4.

McGowen, Tom (2001). Air Raid!: The Bombing Campaign. Brookfield, Connecticut, U.S.A.: Twenty-First Century Books. ISBN 0-7613-1810-0.

Shannon, Donald H. (1976). United States air strategy and doctrine as employed in the strategic bombing of Japan. U.S. Air University, Air War College. ASIN B0006WCQ86.

Smith, Jim; Malcolm Mcconnell (2002). The Last Mission: The Secret History of World War II's Final Battle. Broadway. ISBN 0-7679-0778-7.

Tillman, Barrett (2010). Whirlwind: The Air War Against Japan, 1942–1945. Simon & Schuster. ISBN 978-1-4165-8440-7.

Werrell, Kenneth P. (1998). Blankets of Fire. Smithsonian. ISBN 1-56098-871-1.

Made in United States
Orlando, FL
24 April 2023

32411667R00036